ready. set. bloom.
expanded edition

ready. set. bloom.
expanded edition

a book of poetry
+ mindfulness

words by mairee

All rights reserved.

Copyright © 2022 words by mairee publishing

No part of this publication may be reproduced, distributed, or transmitted in any form or by any means, including photocopying, recording, or other electronic or mechanical methods, without the prior written permission of the publisher, except in the case of brief quotations embodied in critical reviews and certain other noncommercial uses permitted by copyright law.

Ordering Information:
For details, contact
publishing@wordsbymairee.com

Print ISBN: 978-1-7356145-2-6

Printed in the United States of America.

welcome	2
retrospect	3
novel	4
blank	7
malignant	8
lament	9
slant	12
conflicted	13
unconditional	14
impair	17
split	18
favor	19
being	22
sabotage	23
philadelphia	24

passing	27
aesthetic	28
still	29
fleeting	32
weathering	33
stifle	34
alignment	37
grace	38
flowers	39
cycles	42
(un)familiar	43
transparency	44
undo	47
self	48
journey	49
flow	52
scope	53
mairee	54

to mr. nate.
i miss you every day.

cry a really long, hard cry, take a deep breath and try again.

welcome

loving you is like
invitation to heartache.
the door wide open.

mairee 2

retrospect

waiting a lifetime
to unlove you.
when all i wanted,
was to love you
for a lifetime.

novel

i wish i knew love better,
so i could bloom
in everything it is,
not drown
in everything it isn't.

mairee 4

be mindful

use this space to focus on your awareness
in the present moment, and record your reflections.

choosing you can be painful, too.

mairee 6

blank

people will color
your world grey,
then tell you
it was always
black and white.

mairee 7

malignant

with you,
i can't decide if it's the
happiness or heartache
that makes me feel alive,
so i welcome them both
with open arms.

mairee 8

lament

there was a time,
when i was afraid
to love you.
when you loved
me too much.
when i didn't
love myself enough.
when i chose you.
when you chose yourself.

be mindful

use this space to focus on your awareness
in the present moment; and record your reflections.

no regrets.
only lessons.

mairee 11

slant

there are offenses
i have forgiven,
and offered you my heart,
again, with no strings attached.
that you, in turn,
would wear on your
sleeve as a daily reminder
of our undoing.
and that is the difference
between our love.

mairee 12

conflicted

with every breath
i want to run to you,
and from you –
all at once.
i do not know how to love you
any other way.
i do not know how to love you.

mairee 13

unconditional

there are parts of you
i love from the depths of my soul.
and there are others
that unsettle my spirit.
still, i love your whole self
as i do my own.

mairee 14

be mindful

use this space to focus on your awareness
in the present moment; and record your reflections.

learn from it.
heal from it.
grow from it.

mairee 16

impair

sometimes lessons come
gift wrapped in regret.
like lovers who linger in your spirit.
i seemingly have it all together,
so i thought i'd lay it all on the table
to show her i was really falling apart.
but she didn't run.
not right away.
so i gave her a head start.
now she's too far gone.
like the beginning
of our undoing.

mairee 17

split

i tell myself i'm fine.
and sometimes,
for what seems
like a long time,
i really am...
until i'm not.
putting myself
back together.
still, the fear
of falling apart
leaves me broken.

mairee 18

favor

show yourself
the same grace
given to others
for the sins
committed against you.

mairee 19

be mindful

use this space to focus on your awareness
in the present moment; and record your reflections.

*but first,
we are human.*

mairee 21

being

i spend most my days
going through the lost and found,
looking for myself.

mairee 22

sabotage

too many times,
God tried to save me
from a sea of sorrow.
but i ran into the ocean,
to drown in the moment.

mairee 23

philadelphia

i've never felt so lonely as i have
lying in an empty hotel room.
in the middle of a snowstorm.
wrapped in white-washed sheets.
lost in a black hole,
not even i know how to fill.

mairee 24

be mindful

use this space to focus on your awareness
in the present moment; and record your reflections.

*learning
all that
is and isn't
meant for you.*

mairee 26

passing

in a sky full of stars,
does the moon ever
grow lonely
waiting for the sun?

mairee 27

aesthetic

siri, play enough thunder,
track 4 "a case of you".
as i drink the water
painted ombre from
the evening sky,
and the sun takes
its final bow,
i want to hit pause
and freeze this
moment in time.
but then i remember
nights like this
play on repeat in
the memories of you.

mairee 28

still

i wish you could've
loved me then,
the way i love you now.
the way i've always
loved you.
i wish we could
undo the past,
stand still in the present
and free the lovers in between.

mairee 29

be mindful

use this space to focus on your awareness
in the present moment; and record your reflections.

*remember
to be kind
to yourself,
and others.*

mairee 31

fleeting

the days recycle,
like bittersweet split in too.
too bitter, too sweet.

mairee 32

weathering

i forget to show the sun,
who sometimes hides
behind the clouds,
and colors the day gray,
the same grace
i give the moon,
who reveals itself in phases,
before showing up in full form
to light up the night's sky,
neglecting that
sometimes i, too,
hide behind the clouds,
and color the day gray.

mairee 33

stifle

girl, you are dying,
trying not to disappoint
yourself or others?

mairee 34

be mindful

use this space to focus on your awareness
in the present moment; and record your reflections.

every day is a new opportunity to try again.

mairee 36

alignment

there is peace
to be found
in the darkness
of night,
and gratitude
for light
in the morning.

grace

every rising,
every waking breath,
is a gentle reminder
the world isn't over yet.
there's still so much
life to be lived.

mairee 38

flowers

while you were here,
i pray,
more than not,
i celebrated you in life.
in your absence,
i pray,
more than not,
i honor you in spirit.

be mindful

use this space to focus on your awareness
in the present moment; and record your reflections.

just a free spirit trying to make the most of this temporary vessel.

mairee 41

cycles

we are all
falling apart,
and coming together –
at the same time.

mairee 42

(un)familiar

i can't decide
who's changing.
me or them,
all or none
of the above.
you are my only
constant.

mairee 43

transparency

we are all guilty of
blanket lies.
empty promises.
split personalities.
hidden agendas.
only to wake up one day,
and pass familiar faces
in crowds like perfect strangers.

mairee 44

be mindful

use this space to focus on your awareness
in the present moment; and record your reflections.

through all things, love yourself.

mairee 46

undo

little black girl,
when i was your age,
i ran from my skin.
i pray you run free
in yours.

self

through
time and space,
you always
find your way
back to me.

mairee 48

journey

for all i was.
for all i am.
for all i am becoming.
i am grateful.

mairee 49

be mindful

use this space to focus on your awareness
in the present moment; and record your reflections.

standing still.
unknowing which way the wind will blow.
but still standing.

mairee 51

flow

we are not
things to be had.
we are beings
with whom to share
many or few seasons.

mairee 52

scope

journey forward,
or stand still.
alone,
or with others.
in chaos,
or in peace.
in bondage,
or fly free.

mairee 53

mairee

little,
brown girl.
writer.
poet.
night owl.
free spirit.
bipolar.
human.

mairee 54

be mindful

use this space to focus on your awareness
in the present moment; and record your reflections.

everything that blooms has roots ...

Mairee (Mary) studied English at Spelman College and carved a path along the East Coast. She worked as a copy editor, features writer, web producer and social media manager before drifting back to the Midwest. At age 29, she was diagnosed with bipolar depression and developed a passion for spreading mental health awareness in the Black community. She became an advocate for under-represented communities and women and girls of color. And she started writing poetry again. Mairee went back to her roots and the flower within said Ready. Set. Bloom.

www.ingramcontent.com/pod-product-compliance
Lightning Source LLC
Chambersburg PA
CBHW070634050426
42450CB00011B/3186